KEITH
FLOYD

HOT AND SPICY FLOYD

PENGUIN BOOKS

PENGUIN BOOKS

Published by the Penguin Group. Penguin Books Ltd, 27 Wrights Lane, London
w8 5tz, England. Penguin Books USA Inc., 375 Hudson Street, New York,
New York 10014, USA. Penguin Books Australia Ltd, Ringwood, Victoria, Australia.
Penguin Books Canada Ltd, 10 Alcorn Avenue, Toronto, Ontario, Canada m4v 3b2.
Penguin Books (NZ) Ltd, 182 – 190 Wairau Road, Auckland 10, New Zealand · Penguin
Books Ltd, Registered Offices: Harmondsworth, Middlesex, England · These
recipes have been selected from *Floyd on Oz* and *Far Flung Floyd*, first published by
Michael Joseph in 1991 and 1993 respectively. Published in Penguin Books 1992 and
1994 respectively. This edition published 1996. Copyright © Keith Floyd, 1991,
1993. All rights reserved · The moral right of the author has been asserted · Typeset
by Rowland Phototypesetting Ltd, Bury St Edmunds, Suffolk. Printed in England by
Clays Ltd, St Ives plc · Except in the United States of America, this book is sold
subject to the condition that it shall not, by way of trade or otherwise, be lent, re-sold,
hired out, or otherwise circulated without the publisher's prior consent in any form
of binding or cover other than that in which it is published and without a similar
condition including this condition being imposed on the subsequent purchaser ·
10 9 8 7 6 5 4 3 2

CONTENTS

Hot and Spicy Floyd

PORK NOODLE SOUP

A nourishing soup, practically a main course in its own right. And, as long as you already have some roast red pork, see page 34, cooked, it is something you can knock up in literally minutes. All you need are soup spoons and chopsticks and a bottle of rice wine, and you can't go wrong.

SERVES 4

2 litres (3½ pints) chicken Thai soup stock, see page 47

225 g (8 oz) roast red pork, see page 34, or any cooked lean pork, cut into thin slices

1 tablespoon caster sugar

2 tablespoons fish sauce

150 g (6 oz) very thin Chinese dried egg noodles

4 cloves of garlic, finely chopped and fried until crisp

50 g (2 oz) beansprouts

3 crunchy lettuce leaves, finely chopped

To garnish

2 tablespoons coriander leaves, chopped
2 tablespoons roasted peanuts, finely chopped

Bring the chicken stock to the boil in a large pan, then add the pork. Stir in the sugar and fish sauce. Reduce the heat and tip in the egg noodles. Simmer gently for 5 minutes, until tender, then add the garlic, beansprouts and shredded lettuce. Pour into serving bowls and sprinkle with chopped coriander. Serve the chopped peanuts in a separate dish so that people can help themselves.

HOT AND SOUR SEAFOOD SOUP

SERVES 4

1 litre (1¾ pints) chicken stock
1 blade of lemon grass, finely chopped
2.5 cm (1 inch) galingale, finely chopped
2–3 Kaffir lime leaves
450 g (1 lb) king prawns, shelled and deveined, leaving tail ends intact
425 g (15 oz) can straw mushrooms, drained and quartered

fresh coconut slivers (from about ¼ coconut)
1 tablespoon lime juice
2 teaspoons fish sauce
2 teaspoons chilli paste

To garnish

bird's-eye chilli peppers (small and very hot chillies
    also known as dynamite chillies), seeded and
    thinly chopped
coriander leaves

Heat the chicken stock in a pan over a medium heat. Add the lemon grass, galingale and lime leaves. Bring to the boil and throw in the prawns, mushrooms and coconut. Simmer gently until the prawns turn pink and are tender.

Meanwhile, mix together the lime juice, fish sauce and chilli paste. Stir this mixture into the soup when the prawns are cooked. Heat through for a minute or two, then serve sprinkled with the chillies and coriander leaves.

CHICKEN SOUP WITH COCONUT, GINGER AND LEMON GRASS

SERVES 4

150 ml (5 fl oz) chicken stock
2 blades of lemon grass, chopped
4 Kaffir lime leaves, torn in half
5 thin slices of fresh root ginger
500 ml (18 fl oz) coconut milk
225 g (8 oz) boned and skinned chicken breast,
very thinly sliced
4 tablespoons fish sauce
1 tablespoon brown sugar

To garnish

125 ml (4 fl oz) lime juice
1 teaspoon black chilli paste
2 tablespoons coriander leaves, chopped
5 green chilli peppers, seeded and finely
chopped

First, put the stock, lemon grass, lime leaves and ginger in a large pan. Bring to the boil, stirring.

Now add the coconut milk, chicken, fish sauce and sugar and simmer until the chicken slices are tender, about 5–10 minutes.

Put the lime juice and chilli paste in the base of a large serving bowl. Mix them together. Pour the hot soup on top and sprinkle with the coriander and chillies.

THAI FISH CAKES

These are stunningly fresh-flavoured.

SERVES 4

450 g (1 lb) white fish fillets, skinned, boned and cut into chunks – or try mackerel instead
1 blade of lemon grass, bruised and roughly chopped
1 clove of garlic, roughly chopped
1 cm (½ inch) piece of fresh root ginger, roughly chopped
1 red chilli pepper, seeded and chopped
1 tablespoon coriander leaves, chopped
1 teaspoon red curry paste, see page 46
2 tablespoons thick coconut milk
1 tablespoon fish sauce

2 Kaffir lime leaves, roughly chopped
freshly ground black pepper
1 red pepper, seeded and finely chopped
vegetable oil
white wine vinegar
100 g (4 oz) dwarf green beans, chopped

To garnish

coriander leaves, chopped

Whack everything, apart from the red pepper, vinegar and green beans into a food processor or blender and switch on for about 15 seconds or so, to make sure that you have a well-blended, spicy fish mush. Tip it out into a large bowl and mix in the red pepper. Form into fish cakes (you may have to flour your hands to do this).

Heat up some vegetable oil in a frying pan to a depth of about ½ cm (¼ inch) and fry the fish cakes lightly for about 3 minutes on each side, until they are golden-brown, cooked and delicious. Lift out and keep warm. Then into the oil in which you have fried the fish should go a dash of white wine vinegar and the green beans. Fry that up very quickly, pour back over the fish cakes and strew with lots of chopped coriander.

FRIED FISH AND GINGER

To my mind, bass is undoubtedly the king of fish, and a whole, crispy, deep-fried one is a gourmet's treat. But this dish would work equally well with inexpensive dabs or soles. The trick is to drizzle hot oil on to the ginger and spring onions so that they actually cook very lightly.

SERVES 4

2 tablespoons Chinese or ordinary brandy
1 tablespoon light soy sauce
1 teaspoon brown sugar
1 tablespoon sesame oil
1 or 2 whole bass or grey mullet (weighing 900 g
    [2 lb]), scaled, gutted and cleaned
a little plain flour
groundnut or sunflower oil for frying, about 150 ml
    (5 fl oz)
1 tablespoon fresh root ginger, finely chopped
2 tablespoons spring onions, chopped

To garnish

1 red chilli pepper, seeded and finely chopped

Mix together the brandy, soy sauce, sugar and sesame oil. With a sharp knife make several diagonal slashes on both sides of the bass. Lay the fish in a dish and pour over the marinade. Leave in a cool place for about an hour.

Drain the fish and dredge well with flour. Heat the oil until sizzling in a large wok or deep pan. Fry the fish for about 15–20 minutes, until crisp and tender. Carefully lift out the fish and place on a serving dish.

Sprinkle over the ginger and spring onions. Take some hot oil from the wok and drizzle 3 or 4 tablespoons of it over the ginger and spring onions. Garnish with the chilli.

STEAMED BASS OR GROUPER WITH CHILLI SAUCE

A firm fish like bass, or mullet, is perfect for steaming – and especially with these tangy flavours from the herbs and spices. The steaming process really does enhance the flavours.

SERVES 4

1 or 2 whole bass or grouper (weighing 700 g [1½ lb]), scaled, gutted and cleaned
2 tablespoons rice wine (or use dry sherry)

4 green chilli peppers, seeded and finely chopped
2 spring onions, very finely chopped
2 cloves of garlic, crushed or finely chopped
2 tablespoons fresh root ginger, grated
1 small onion, finely chopped
2 blades of lemon grass, bruised and finely chopped
3 tablespoons fish sauce
60 ml (2 fl oz) lime juice
2 tablespoons basil leaves, chopped
salt
white pepper

Wash and dry the fish. With a sharp knife make half-a-dozen slashes over the skin of the fish. Mix together all the remaining ingredients and spread over the fish. Steam on a perforated tray in a large wok that has a domed lid for about 25 minutes, or until the flesh is firm but still moist and tender. Alternatively, you could use a big bamboo steamer or a fish kettle. To serve, pass round the chilli sauce separately.

Chilli Sauce
10 green chilli peppers, seeded and chopped
4 cloves of garlic, chopped
120 ml (4 fl oz) fish sauce
150 ml (5 fl oz) lime or lemon juice

Put the four ingredients in your blender or food processor and whizz well. It's as easy as that!

FISH STEAMED WITH CELERY

This is a fine way of injecting some flavour into the humbler species of fish like whiting or small pollock. But if the pocket permits, go for bass or red mullet.

SERVES 2–3

5 stalks of celery
1 whole saltwater fish (550 g [1¼ lb]), whiting, pollock, bass or red mullet, scaled, cleaned and gutted
salt
freshly ground black pepper
2 green chilli peppers, seeded and finely chopped
2 cloves of garlic, finely chopped
4 spring onions, finely chopped
1 tablespoon fish sauce
1 wineglass dry white wine

It is important first to remove the 'strings' from the celery, so there are no fibrous bits on the outside. Cut the celery into thin strips about 7.5 cm (3 inches) long. Be careful not to cut the celery too coarsely or it will take longer to cook than the fish.

With a sharp knife, make several deep slashes on each side of the fish, then rub in the salt and pepper. Put the fish in a steamer or fish kettle, add the celery, then sprinkle and pour on the remaining ingredients. You could also steam the fish on a perforated tray in a large wok with a lid. Steam until the fish is firm but still moist, about 15 minutes.

STEAMED FISH CURRY WITH HERBS

This is a splendid curry which I cooked in my Thai chum Chom's house, which is a beautiful hardwood bungalow set on stilts at the edge of a rice paddy field some twenty miles east of Bangkok. The great advantage of steaming is that it is a gentle process and it doesn't overcook or damage the fish. I commend it to the house!

SERVES 4

spinach or blanched cabbage leaves
1–2 sprigs basil leaves
1–2 sprigs mint leaves
2 eggs, beaten

300 ml (10 fl oz) coconut cream
2 tablespoons fish sauce
3 tablespoons red curry paste, see page 46
*450 g (1 lb) bass (or other firm white fish), sliced
    thinly*

To garnish

4 Kaffir lime leaves, chopped
*1 red and 1 green chilli pepper, seeded and finely
    chopped*
1 tablespoon coriander leaves, roughly chopped

Use a deep dish that will fit in a steamer. Line the dish with either spinach or blanched cabbage leaves and the basil and mint leaves.

Mix together the eggs, coconut cream, fish sauce and red curry paste and stir well.

Fold in the fish and pour this mixture into the lined dish. Sprinkle the lime leaves, chillies and coriander on top. Cover with foil or a heatproof plate. Steam for 15–20 minutes from the time the steamer water has started to boil. Serve from the bowl with rice.

CHILLI PRAWNS

Prawns come in all shapes and sizes in Malaysia, from shrimp-size ones as small as your fingernail to monsters about a foot long. They are cheap and plentiful and I particularly enjoyed this little snack that my friend chef Razak prepared for me one breakfast-time in the Tanjong Jara beach resort.

SERVES 4

4 tablespoons groundnut oil
1 tablespoon onion, grated
1 tablespoon fresh root ginger, minced or grated
1 small onion, chopped
2 shallots, chopped
at least 450 g (1 lb) tomatoes, skinned and chopped
pinch of ground saffron
2 tablespoons chilli sauce, see page 11
1 tablespoon ground turmeric
700 g (1½ lb) large cooked prawns, peeled, heads
    removed and tails left intact

To garnish
cucumber, sliced or cubed

Heat half the oil in a pan. Add the grated onion, ginger, chopped onion and shallots and cook gently for around 10 minutes. Pop in the tomatoes, saffron and chilli sauce and cover. Cook for about 15 minutes.

Sprinkle the turmeric over the prawns. Heat the remaining oil in a wok or frying pan and fry the prawns briskly for about 2 minutes. Drain and arrange on a serving dish. Add a little water to the sauce if necessary to give a pouring consistency. Heat through, then pour over the prawns or serve separately and garnish with the cucumber.

PRAWN STIR-FRY

You could serve this as a yummy starter or with rice and/ or salad as a main course – lunch or dinner.

SERVES 4

450 g (1 lb) large peeled prawns
2 tablespoons sesame oil
1 bunch of spring onions, trimmed and chopped
1 small handful of coriander leaves, finely chopped
2 cloves of garlic, finely chopped
grated zest and juice of 1 lemon

5 cm (2 inch) piece of fresh root ginger, grated
juice of 2 limes
1 tablespoon dark soy sauce
salt
freshly ground black pepper

To garnish

coriander leaves

Remove the back vein from the prawns by making a shallow incision along the top of each prawn and removing the white or black intestinal vein with the point of a knife.

Heat the oil in a large frying pan or wok and stir-fry the prawns for about 20 seconds, then add the spring onions, coriander, garlic, lemon zest and juice, and ginger. Stir-fry for 2–3 minutes, then squeeze over the lime juice and add the soy sauce. Season to taste with salt and pepper and serve immediately, garnished with the coriander leaves.

RED-HOT SCALLOPS

I have often stated that the crayfish, the saltwater variety that is, is absolutely my favourite shellfish. I have now decided that scallops are my most favourite crustacean, arthropod, call them what you will, in the entire world. And here is a superb recipe.

SERVES 4

12–16 scallops, depending on size, removed from
   shells and washed
4 tablespoons red curry paste, see page 46
2 tablespoons vegetable oil
2 cloves of garlic, finely chopped
2 red chilli peppers, seeded and finely chopped
2 tablespoons fish sauce
1 tablespoon caster sugar

To garnish
1 large handful of basil leaves

Discard the crescent-shaped muscle from each scallop, then mix together the scallops and the curry paste in a bowl (not aluminium) and leave to marinate for at least 15 minutes. Heat the oil in a frying pan or wok and stir-fry the garlic until golden. Tip in the scallops with the curry paste and the chillies and stir-fry for 2 minutes. Add the fish sauce and sugar and cook, stirring, for 1 more minute. Taste and adjust seasonings – add more fish sauce, sugar or chilli if necessary. When the scallops are tender and have just whitened (about

1 minute more – do not overcook scallops or they will be tough), stir in most of the basil, then remove from the heat. Serve on a bed of stir-fried *pak choy*, garnish with the remaining basil and accompany with a bowl of plain, boiled rice.

FRIED MUSSELS

These simple, spicy mussels are finger-lickin', dead good! I once bought a bowl of them from a floating kitchen set up in a little twelve-foot punt, as I was paddling around the Bangkok Floating Market on Sunday morning, as one does.

SERVES 2 – 3

   3 tablespoons groundnut oil
   3 shallots, *finely chopped*
   3 cloves of garlic, *finely chopped*
   1 tablespoon soy bean paste
   1 red chilli pepper, *seeded and chopped*
   2.5 cm (1 inch) piece of fresh root ginger,
      chopped
   700 g (1½ lb) mussels in shells, *cleaned, bearded*
      and rinsed
   1 teaspoon brown sugar

Heat the oil in a large pan and lightly brown the shallots and garlic for around 5 minutes. Add the soy bean paste and mix this in well before adding the chilli, ginger and mussels. Stir-fry these over a high heat for a minute before sprinkling on the sugar.

Cover the pan and cook over a high heat for about 5 minutes, shaking the pan frequently until the mussels have opened and released their juices. Discard any that remain obstinately shut or you may regret it.

Transfer the mussels to individual bowls and strain over the cooking liquid.

TURMERIC CHICKEN

This is a lovely, creamy, nutty Vietnamese-style curry that you can make as hot and as spicy as you wish merely by adding a little chopped chilli pepper. Or, if you wish, leave the chilli out. And the gentle flavours of turmeric and coconut milk make it a dish to drool over.

SERVES 4

2 tablespoons vegetable oil
1 large onion, chopped
3 cloves of garlic, finely chopped

1 small green chilli pepper, seeded and finely
  chopped (optional)
450 g (1 lb) boned chicken meat, cut into bite-sized
  pieces
1½ tablespoons ground turmeric
generous pinch of salt
1 tablespoon lemon grass, finely chopped
1 teaspoon bean sauce
500 ml (18 fl oz) coconut milk

To garnish

roasted peanuts, chopped
coriander leaves, chopped

Heat the oil in a large frying pan or wok, add the
onion, garlic and chilli, if using, and then the chicken.
Stir-fry for about 3–4 minutes, until the meat changes
colour. Pop in the remaining ingredients, apart from 3
tablespoons of coconut milk. Cook over a moderate heat
for 30 minutes or until the chicken is tender. Stir from
time to time, adding extra water if necessary to prevent
burning.

Remove from the heat when the chicken is cooked and the
sauce has reduced and thickened. Stir through the reserved
coconut milk. Sprinkle with the chopped roasted peanuts

and coriander and serve with mounds of plain, boiled rice
or cellophane noodles.

STIR-FRIED CHICKEN WITH GREEN CURRY
PASTE AND BASIL

This simple dish is an example of the cross-fertilization
between Thai and Chinese kitchens. We first ate it at a
simple street stall on Ko Samui. We so thoroughly enjoyed
it and had such attentive service from some extremely
beautiful Thai waitresses that, after we had paid the bill,
we presented them with a large tip saying, as you would in
England, 'This is for you.'

One girl became rather excited and said, 'You want me?'
Slight confusion there, but we managed to dissuade her from
packing her bags and coming with us. It was she who said to
us before we left, 'In Thailand, one smile makes two.'

SERVES 4

3 tablespoons vegetable oil
3 tablespoons green curry paste, see page 46
450 g (1 lb) boned chicken, sliced thinly
60 ml (2 fl oz) coconut milk

3 tablespoons brown sugar

3 tablespoons fish sauce

3 tablespoons mixed red and green chilli peppers,
  seeded and chopped

2 fistfuls basil leaves

To garnish

4 tablespoons coconut cream

Heat the oil in a wok or large frying pan. Stir in the green curry paste. Throw in the chicken and stir-fry quickly over a high heat for 2–3 minutes. Add the coconut milk, sugar, fish sauce and chilli peppers. Cook for 5 minutes, stirring well. Just before serving, toss in the basil leaves. Pop a spoonful of coconut cream on top of each serving. This is excellent with steamed rice.

THAI CHICKEN CURRY

One sunny autumnal day at a cricket ground in Romsey, Victoria, I had the dubious distinction of playing cricket with Frank Tyson. Or, rather, he played cricket, I just got bowled out.

However, I was able to restore some of my dented

sporting pride by hitting them for six – ho ho! – with this frightfully simple, terribly delicious little curry.

SERVES 4

2 tablespoons vegetable oil

4 × 150 g (6 oz) boneless chicken breasts, skinned
   and cut into small strips

450 ml (16 fl oz) thick coconut milk

2 medium green chilli peppers, seeded and chopped

2 tablespoons green curry paste, see page 46

2 blades of lemon grass, bruised and finely chopped

2 tablespoons coriander leaves, chopped

1 tablespoon basil or mint leaves, chopped

1 tablespoon fish sauce

salt

freshly ground black pepper

To garnish

coriander leaves

Heat the oil in a large pan and fry the chicken pieces for 3–4 minutes, until sealed. Pour in most of the coconut milk and add the fresh chillies, green curry paste and lemon grass. Bring to the boil, then reduce the heat and simmer gently for 15–20 minutes.

Tip in the coriander, basil or mint and fish sauce. Stir in the remaining coconut milk and bubble for 5 more minutes. Check the seasoning and add a little salt and pepper if necessary. Serve with plain, boiled rice and garnish with some coriander leaves.

VIETNAMESE FRIED CHICKEN

SERVES 3–4

2 tablespoons light soy sauce
2 tablespoons fish sauce
freshly ground black pepper
2 teaspoons brown sugar
5 cloves of garlic, crushed and ground to a paste
4 shallots, finely chopped
900 g (2 lb) chicken, cut into 8 pieces
a little plain flour
groundnut oil

Mix together the soy and fish sauces. Add black pepper to taste. Stir in the sugar, garlic and shallots. No salt is needed as the fish sauce is salty enough.

Rub the mixture all over the chicken pieces and leave in a cool place to marinate for at least an hour.

Remove the chicken and sprinkle the pieces with a little flour. Heat about 5 cm (2 inches) oil in a deep-fryer or wok, and deep-fry the chicken pieces a few at a time until tender and golden with lovely crispy skins – about 8–10 minutes.

Remove the pieces as they are cooked, drain on kitchen paper and keep warm. Serve with boiled rice and your favourite dipping sauce.

DUCK SALAD WITH HOT AND SOUR DRESSING

SERVES 4

4 duck breast fillets, roasted or grilled and thinly
   sliced
crisp lettuce leaves
2 shallots, finely chopped
4 spring onions, finely chopped
matchstick batons of cucumber and celery
3 tablespoons fish sauce
1–2 tablespoons lime juice
2 cloves of garlic, crushed or finely chopped
1 red and 1 green chilli pepper, seeded and very
   finely chopped
1 teaspoon palm or demerara sugar

To garnish

celery leaves
chilli pepper, seeded and chopped
spring onions, chopped

Arrange the slices of duck on a bed of lettuce on a serving dish. Sprinkle over the shallots, spring onions, cucumber and celery.

To make the dressing, put the fish sauce, lime juice, garlic, chillies and sugar into a small pan, and heat through gently. The actual amount of ingredients is just a guide and you can experiment with it until it is to your liking. Pour the warm dressing over the salad and garnish with the celery leaves, chopped chilli and chopped spring onions.

DYNAMITE DRUNKEN BEEF

This is an awesomely hot creation of my Thai chum Chom, which takes its name from the small, very hot chillies known as bird's-eye or dynamite chillies. (Nothing to do with Captain Birdseye, by the way!)

SERVES 4

2 cloves of garlic
2.5 cm (1 inch) piece of galingale, chopped

2 shallots, chopped

2 very hot chilli peppers (preferably bird's-eye),
seeded and chopped

2 tablespoons groundnut oil

700 g (1½ lb) lean beef, such as fillet, thinly sliced

a few fresh green peppercorns

1 red and 1 green chilli pepper, seeded and sliced
lengthways

2–3 Kaffir lime leaves, torn

100 g (4 oz) green beans, cut into 2.5 cm (1 inch)
lengths

1 tablespoon fish sauce

1 teaspoon palm or demerara sugar

2 teaspoons distilled malt vinegar or rice vinegar

whisky, to 'flame'

about 8 basil leaves

Using a pestle and mortar or small blender, pound or mix together the garlic, galingale, shallots and chillies.

Heat the oil in a wok or frying pan and fry the pounded garlic mixture for a few minutes. Add the beef, peppercorns, chillies, lime leaves and green beans. Stir-fry over a high heat for about 5 minutes. The vegetables should still be crisp and bright-coloured. Pop in the fish sauce, brown sugar and vinegar and mix well.

Pour in a generous tot of the whisky and set it alight to 'flame' the dish. Reduce the heat and stir in the basil leaves just before serving.

FRIED BEEF WITH CASHEW NUTS

This is an example of Thais taking a basic Chinese dish and refining it to suit their love of fiery food.

I cooked this on Ko Samui and was able to use the fresh cashew nuts that are grown on the island. And their oily, nutty, crunchy texture goes really well with the tender strips of beef.

SERVES 4

2 tablespoons groundnut oil or sesame oil

2.5 cm (1 inch) piece of fresh root ginger, finely chopped or grated

1 onion, halved and sliced

1 clove of garlic, finely chopped

450 g (1 lb) lean beef, such as fillet, thinly sliced and cut into strips

ground white pepper

1 teaspoon brown sugar

2 tablespoons light soy sauce
1 small green and 1 small red pepper, seeded and
   thinly sliced lengthways
3 spring onions, sliced diagonally
2 stalks celery, chopped
about 6 pieces of dried Chinese black mushrooms,
   soaked, drained and chopped (optional)
4 tablespoons roasted cashew nuts
2–4 tablespoons beef stock

To garnish

celery leaves

Heat the oil in a wok or deep frying-pan. Add the ginger,
onion and garlic and stir-fry over a high heat for 2–3
minutes. Throw in the beef and stir-fry for a further 2–3
minutes, until browned. Season to taste with the pepper,
sugar and soy sauce.

Add the green and red peppers, spring onions, celery,
mushrooms and nuts. Pour in a little beef stock and stir-fry
for about 3 minutes. Garnish with celery leaves, if you like.
Serve with white rice noodles.

SPICY BEEF SATAY

The bamboo satay sticks needed for this recipe can be bought from good cookshops. Soaking them in water first prevents them from burning.

SERVES 4

450 g (1 lb) rump steak, cut into very thin strips
1 tablespoon light soy sauce
1 teaspoon sesame oil
2 teaspoons red curry paste, see page 46
2 tablespoons peanut butter or sesame (tahini)
    paste
2 tablespoons dry sherry
2 tablespoons vegetable oil

Mix together the steak, soy sauce and sesame oil in a large bowl (not aluminium) and leave to marinate for 15 minutes or so. Soak about a dozen bamboo satay sticks in water.

Thread 3 or 4 slices of beef on to each satay stick. Leave 2·5 cm (1 inch) at the pointed end of each stick without meat.

Stir together the curry paste, peanut butter or sesame paste, and sherry in a bowl and use to baste the beef. Brush well with the oil and pop under a preheated hot grill. Cook for 1–2 minutes on each side. Serve with plain, boiled rice and some satay sauce, see below.

PS If you like, beat the steak out thinly between sheets of greaseproof paper with a meat mallet or rolling pin before cutting it up. This will tenderize it.

Satay Sauce

6 tablespoons crunchy peanut butter
1 tablespoon dark soy sauce
1 tablespoon fish sauce
1 small onion, roughly chopped
1 tablespoon brown sugar
150 ml (5 fl oz) coconut milk
½ teaspoon cayenne pepper
pinch of salt

Chuck all the ingredients into a food processor or blender and whizz together until smooth. Pour into a small pan and heat gently until just boiling. Pour into a bowl to serve with the satays.

MALAYSIAN BEEF CURRY

SERVES 4

2 tablespoons groundnut oil
1 teaspoon ground cinnamon
1 teaspoon ground cumin
1 teaspoon star anise, chopped
2 whole cardamoms, crushed
4 whole cloves
2 curry or bay leaves
1 tablespoon fresh root ginger, grated
6 shallots, chopped
450 g (1 lb) lean stewing steak, cubed
2 tablespoons mild curry powder
3 medium potatoes, peeled and cubed
3 green chilli peppers, seeded and finely chopped
425 ml (¾ pint) coconut milk
salt
juice of 1 lime

Heat the oil in a large pan and sauté the cinnamon, cumin, star anise, cardamoms, cloves and curry or bay leaves for a minute. Stir in the ginger and shallots and cook for another couple of minutes. Pop in the meat and cook until browned.

Stir in the curry powder, potatoes and chillies. Add the coconut milk. Cover and simmer for about 45 minutes, or until the meat is tender. Stir well and often during cooking. Season with salt and add lime juice to taste just before serving. Fish out the bay or curry leaves.

ROAST RED PORK

SERVES 4

1 kg (2–2¼ lb) pork fillet or boneless pork loin, trimmed

For the marinade

½ teaspoon red food colouring, mixed with 3 tablespoons cold water

1 tablespoon fish sauce

1 tablespoon light soy sauce

2 tablespoons hoisin sauce

1 tablespoon dry sherry

1 tablespoon caster sugar

2.5 cm (1 inch) piece of fresh root ginger, grated

3 cloves of garlic, chopped

1 tablespoon sesame oil

½ teaspoon ground fennel or fennel seeds, or 3 star
    anise, crushed

To garnish

coriander leaves

Pop all the ingredients for the marinade into a food processor or blender and whizz to a smooth paste. Put the pork and marinade into a large plastic bag, tie securely and leave the meat to marinate for at least a couple of hours, but preferably overnight. Turn the bag occasionally to make sure that the meat is well covered with the marinade.

Remove the pork from the plastic bag and put it on a rack over a roasting tin, reserving the marinade for basting. Cook the pork in a preheated oven, 230°C/450°F (gas mark 8), for 10 minutes. Reduce the heat to 180°C/350°F (gas mark 4), and continue to roast for 45 minutes, basting from time to time. Allow the meat to rest in a warm place for 10–15 minutes or so before carving.

The pork can be served warm, sliced thinly and arranged on a flat serving dish, garnished with coriander leaves and served with rice. Alternatively, it can be used in many soups and stir-fries.

VEGETABLE CURRY SALAD

SERVES 4–6

4 carrots, chopped
100 g (4 oz) white cabbage, chopped
225 g (8 oz) baby sweetcorn
225 g (8 oz) asparagus tips
100 g (4 oz) green beans, cut into 2.5 cm (1 inch)
  pieces
1 aubergine, peeled and diced
225 g (8 oz) beansprouts, well rinsed
100 g (4 oz) button mushrooms, chopped

For the Sweet and Sour Curry Sauce

2 tablespoons coconut oil
1 tablespoon red curry paste
2 tablespoons coconut cream
1 tablespoon light soy sauce
1 teaspoon brown sugar
1 tablespoon tamarind water
salt
1 teaspoon ground coriander
1 teaspoon ground cumin

2 tablespoons roasted peanuts, finely chopped

To garnish

3 shallots, chopped and deep-fried until golden
3–4 cloves of garlic, chopped and deep-fried until
   golden
1 tablespoon toasted sesame seeds

Blanch the carrots, cabbage, sweetcorn, asparagus, green beans and aubergine in boiling water. Drain. Arrange the blanched vegetables in a salad bowl, together with the bean-sprouts and mushrooms.

Heat the oil in a pan and add the red curry paste. Stir for a minute to release the flavours. Carefully stir in the coconut cream, soy sauce, sugar, tamarind water, salt, coriander, cumin and peanuts. Pour over the vegetables.

Sprinkle with the deep-fried shallots, garlic and the toasted sesame seeds.

MALAYSIAN VEGETABLE STEW

One for you vegetarians here, with this Malaysian stew.
Delicious on its own, or with rice noodles.

SERVES 4

3 shallots, finely chopped
1 clove of garlic, finely chopped
1 green chilli pepper, seeded and finely chopped
7 tablespoons cold water
1 teaspoon ground turmeric
1 teaspoon ground ginger
1 blade of lemon grass, bruised
salt
2 potatoes, peeled and quartered
450 ml (16 fl oz) vegetable, chicken or beef stock
100 g (4 oz) white cabbage, coarsely chopped
½ small marrow, peeled, seeded and cut into chunks
50 g (2 oz) creamed coconut, chopped

Put the shallots, garlic, chilli, water, turmeric, ginger and
lemon grass into a large pan. Add a little salt and bring to
the boil. Bubble for 2 minutes, then whack in the potatoes
38 and half the stock. Bring to the boil, cover and simmer for

5 minutes. Tip in the cabbage, marrow and remaining stock, return to the boil and simmer, covered, for 5–6 minutes, or until the vegetables are just tender. Add the creamed coconut and stir until dissolved. Check the seasoning, fish out and discard the lemon grass and serve with noodles.

STIR-FRIED SPINACH WITH GARLIC

SERVES 4

900 g (2 lb) spinach, thoroughly washed and
*   trimmed*
2 tablespoons peanut oil
6 cloves of garlic, finely chopped
1 tablespoon fish sauce
knob of butter
freshly ground black pepper

Gently dry the spinach in a salad spinner or in a clean tea towel. Heat the oil in a large wok or frying pan, add the garlic and stir-fry for 1–2 minutes, until golden. Add the spinach and cook for 2–3 minutes. Stir in the fish sauce and the butter and liberally twist some pepper over the lot.

THAI FRIED NOODLES

SERVES 4

4 tablespoons groundnut oil

2 shallots, finely chopped

1 egg

*100 g (4 oz) medium flat noodles, soaked in water
for 20 minutes until soft, then drained*

2 tablespoons lime or lemon juice

1 tablespoon fish sauce

½–1 teaspoon tamarind concentrate

1 teaspoon brown sugar

*100 g (4 oz) beancurd (tofu), finely chopped and
deep-fried*

1 tablespoon roasted peanuts, chopped

*1 tablespoon whole dried prawns, ground or
pounded – rinse before use*

*1 tablespoon preserved radish (Tang Chi), finely
chopped*

25 g (1 oz) beansprouts

*chopped Chinese chives (or the green stalks of
spring onions)*

To Garnish

1 tablespoon roasted peanuts, chopped
1 tablespoon whole dried prawns, ground or
pounded
2 red chilli peppers, seeded and chopped
sprigs of coriander

In a wok or frying pan, heat the oil, add the shallots and fry for about 10 minutes, until tender and golden brown. Break the egg into the wok and stir quickly for a couple of seconds. Throw in the noodles and stir well. Mix well with the shallots and egg, scraping down the sides of the wok.

Add the lime or lemon juice, fish sauce, tamarind concentrate, sugar, beancurd, peanuts, dried prawns, the preserved radish, the beansprouts and chives. Stir-fry quickly for a couple of minutes. Serve sprinkled with the peanuts, dried prawns and the chilli and coriander.

STICKY RICE WITH CHICKEN AND PORK

SERVES 6

2½ tablespoons light soy sauce
2 tablespoons oyster sauce

1 tablespoon brown sugar
groundnut oil
225 g (8 oz) chicken breast fillets, skinned and
*   cut into bite-sized pieces*
350 g (12 oz) lean pork, diced
50 g (2 oz) shiitake mushrooms, chopped
1 tablespoon cornflour (optional)
450 g (1 lb) sticky rice (short or round grain)
*   soaked in water overnight, then drained*
salt
freshly ground black pepper

To garnish
coriander leaves, chopped

Put the soy sauce, oyster sauce and sugar into a bowl and
mix together. Pop about three-quarters of this mixture into
a large bowl and add the chicken and pork. Coat well in the
mixture.

Heat a little oil in a wok or large frying pan and cook the
chicken and pork for about 5 minutes until golden. Add the
mushrooms and a little water. Cover and simmer for about
20 minutes, until the pork and chicken are tender. If the
sauce is very thin, thicken it with the cornflour mixed with
42 a little water.

Mix the drained rice with the remaining soy sauce mixture and seasoning.

Put some chicken and pork mixture into the bottom of individual heatproof bowls. Top up to the halfway mark with rice. Steam over boiling water for about 30 minutes, until the rice is cooked. You can either do this by putting the bowls into a bamboo steamer and setting this on a rack in a large wok or placing them in a normal steamer. Remember to keep the water topped up. Turn out and sprinkle with coriander leaves.

THAI FRIED RICE

A colourful and appetizing dish with bite-sized pieces of meat. Make the garnish as simple or elaborate as you like.

SERVES 4

3 tablespoons vegetable oil
2 large onions, finely chopped
2 cloves of garlic, crushed
1 teaspoon caster sugar
1 tablespoon red curry paste, see page 46, or 1
    tablespoon Tabasco sauce

450 g (*1 lb*) mixture of peeled prawns, sliced pork,
    beef, chicken or ham
3 eggs, beaten
1 kg (*2–2¼ lb*) cooked long-grain rice
2 tablespoons fish sauce
1 red or green pepper, seeded and finely chopped
50 g (*2 oz*) dwarf green beans, chopped
2 tomatoes, skinned and chopped
3–4 spring onions, trimmed and chopped, or 2
    shallots, chopped

To garnish

coriander leaves
spring onion curls or cucumber slices

Heat the oil in a large frying pan or wok and stir-fry the
onions and garlic for 3–4 minutes, until golden. Stir in the
caster sugar and red curry paste. (If using Tabasco, add this
later.) Tip in the prawns and sliced meat, stir through and
cook for 30 seconds or so. Push to one side of the pan, add
a few more drops of oil, then pour in the eggs. Allow to set
for a few seconds, then scramble them. Add the rice and
stir-fry the lot until thoroughly heated, about 2–3 minutes.
(Add the Tabasco now, if using.) Add the fish sauce, pepper,

beans, tomatoes and spring onions or shallots. Cook for a couple of minutes, then serve with the garnishes.

COCONUT RICE

Who wants plain rice all the time – not me!

SERVES 4

450 g (1 lb) long-grain rice, thoroughly rinsed
1 onion, chopped
75 g (3 oz) creamed coconut, roughly chopped
½ teaspoon salt
few drops vegetable oil or a knob of butter

Measure the rice in cups and transfer to a large pan. For each cup of rice, add 2 cups of water to the pan. Stir in the onion, coconut, salt and a few drops of oil or a good knob of butter. Bring to the boil, then reduce the heat to low. Cover and cook for about 20 minutes, or until all the liquid has been absorbed and the rice is tender and fluffy. Serve hot with curry.

   PS For a delicious, spicy change, why not add a piece of cinnamon stick, a couple of cloves and cardamom pods and a bay leaf. Remember to fish out and discard them before serving.

GREEN OR RED CURRY PASTE

Of course, when I made this curry paste for the Thai chicken curry, see page 23, I sat up in my hotel room the night before grinding it with a mortar and pestle, while the rest of the crew were out on the town. But what you could do is whack the whole lot through a spice grinder or coffee mill.

MAKES ENOUGH FOR 5–8 CURRIES

1 teaspoon cumin seeds or 1 teaspoon ground cumin

1 tablespoon coriander seeds or 1 tablespoon ground coriander

1 whole nutmeg or 2 teaspoons ground nutmeg

12 black peppercorns or 1½ teaspoons ground black pepper

2.5 cm (1 inch) piece of dried galingale, chopped, or 1 tablespoon dried galingale powder

1 blade of lemon grass, finely chopped

10 whole green chilli peppers, stemmed and finely chopped, or for red curry paste 12 medium dried red chilli peppers, seeded and chopped

grated zest of 1 lime

5 cloves of garlic, chopped
4 shallots, finely chopped
1 teaspoon shrimp paste or anchovy essence
2 tablespoons coriander roots, finely chopped
1 teaspoon salt
4 tablespoons vegetable oil

If using whole spices, put the cumin and coriander seeds, nutmeg, peppercorns, dried galingale and lemon grass into an electric spice mill or coffee grinder and grind to a powder. Alternatively, grind them using a mortar and pestle. Put the ground spices into a processor or blender and add all the remaining ingredients. Whizz until a smooth paste is formed.

Keep the paste in a screw-topped jar and store in the refrigerator for up to 1 month. Use in Thai recipes.

THAI SOUP STOCK

A terrifically versatile, basic stock. Freeze in ice-cube trays or little pots for emergency or impromptu use – or for sheer convenience.

MAKES 1.5–2 LITRES (2½–3½ PINTS)

2.25 litres (4 pints) cold water
700 g (1½ lb) chicken, beef, pork or fish bones,
    depending on the flavour of the stock you need
2 sticks of celery, chopped
2 onions, chopped
2 coriander roots, chopped
4 Kaffir lime leaves
2.5 cm (1 inch) piece of fresh root ginger, chopped
salt
freshly ground black pepper

Put all the ingredients into a very large pan. Bring to the boil, then reduce the heat and simmer, covered, for about 1 hour, skimming the fat from the surface from time to time.

Strain through a fine sieve and discard all but the stock, then strain again, lining the sieve with muslin to achieve a clear liquid. Cool and refrigerate, then skim off any fat from the surface. Use within 2 days, or freeze and keep for up to 3 months. Use in Thai soup recipes.

GLOSSARY

Beancurd Often called by its Japanese name tofu, this is made from puréed and pressed soy beans and has a texture like soft cheese, but a bland flavour. It is, though, extremely useful in absorbing the flavour of other ingredients. Beancurd is normally sold in small, firm blocks in its liquid, which is discarded before using. There is a soft junket variety that is best used in soups. Solid beancurd for stir-frying should be carefully cut into cubes or shreds with a sharp knife. Too much stirring can cause it to disintegrate. Look for it in Oriental shops, health food stores and some supermarkets.

Bean Sauce Known as yellow bean and brown or black bean sauce as well, bean sauce is made from crushed yellow soy beans, mixed to a paste with flour, vinegar, spices and salt. It tastes quite salty, but has a spicy, aromatic flavour. Sold in jars and cans and available in large supermarkets under popular brand names – look in the Oriental foods section.

Chilli Paste These roast ground chillies mixed with oil and sold in small jars can be bought in Oriental shops. They 49 come in varying makes and colours and are often labelled 'Ground Chillies in Oil'.

Coconut Milk You can buy coconut milk in cans from Oriental shops or large supermarkets and this is by far the easiest to use. Make sure it is unsweetened. Otherwise, coconut milk is made by soaking the flesh of fresh coconut in boiling water or milk, then extracting the liquid. It is also possible to use creamed coconut (see below), or dried, unsweetened (desiccated) coconut available from health food shops. Use ordinary silver-top milk to make the coconut milk rather than water – it will produce a much richer, creamier result. It will also produce the heavier coconut cream that will rise to the surface and can be skimmed off to use in various recipes.

To make about 250 ml (9 fl oz) coconut milk, heat 500 ml (18 fl oz) milk until almost boiling. Remove from the heat and stir in 225 g (8 oz) grated fresh coconut or unsweetened desiccated coconut. Allow to cool to room temperature, stirring from time to time. Pour through a sieve, using the back of a spoon to extract as much liquid as possible. If you need coconut cream, allow to stand so that this rises to the surface, then skim.

You can also use the leftover coconut again for further extractions, but these really will be thinner and less flavoursome. Treat coconut milk as you would fresh milk – keep in the refrigerator and use within a couple of days.

Creamed Coconut You can buy blocks of creamed coconut, which are more concentrated than coconut milk from Oriental shops or large supermarkets. To make coconut milk from it, chop or grate, say, 75 g (3 oz) and then heat gently with 175 ml (6 fl oz) water stirring frequently until dissolved.

Coriander Coriander roots have a more intense flavour than the leaves and are frequently used in Asian cooking, either finely chopped or pounded, in marinades, curry pastes and so on. They may be bought in Middle Eastern or specialist stores and usually come with leaves and stalks attached. The roots should be rinsed and dried and kept in an airtight container in the fridge where they will stay fresh for several days. If the roots are unavailable, substitute coriander stalks.

Curry Leaves These leaves are rather like bay leaves but thinner and not so leathery. They are olive green and very aromatic. They may be obtained, fresh or dried, all year round from Asian shops. They may be minced, torn or left whole, according to the recipe.

Fish Sauce This is a fundamental flavouring for Vietnamese and Thai cooking and there isn't really a substitute. It is available in bottles from Chinese and Oriental stores. Fish sauce is salty and comes in several varieties such as anchovy, prawn and squid. The colour and flavour will vary slightly according to type.

Galingale In Thailand, galingale nearly replaces ginger as a spice. It is related to ginger, but has a less pungent flavour. Galingale can be bought fresh from Oriental stores and needs to be peeled like ginger before slicing. It is also sold as a powder and dried – soak dried pieces before using and fish out and discard before serving. When substituting dried for fresh galingale in a recipe, use 1 dried slice or 1 teaspoon powder for each 1 cm (½ inch) fresh specified in the recipe. You could also substitute with half the amount of fresh root ginger, which will give a more pungent flavour.

Hoisin Sauce Dark reddish-brown in colour, this thick sauce is sweet and spicy. It is made from soy beans, wheat flour, salt, sugar, vinegar, garlic, chilli and sesame oil. It is used as a dip for marinades and other recipes. Sold in jars and tins, it is available from Chinese grocers, delicatessens and some supermarkets. Once opened, it will keep in a screw-topped jar in the refrigerator for several months.

Kaffir Lime Leaves The glossy, dark green lime leaves give dishes a lovely lemony-lime flavour. You can find them, fresh or dried, in Oriental shops. The fresh lime leaves keep well and can be frozen. If Kaffir lime leaves are not readily available, use 1 teaspoon finely grated lime peel for 1 lime leaf.

Lemon Grass This looks a little like a hard-skinned, elongated spring onion, with fibrous, grey-green leaves. It adds an intense, but not sharp, lemon flavour and scent to cooking. You can buy it fairly easily from the greengrocer's sections in supermarkets and from specialist stores. When a recipe specifies chopped or sliced, then the bulky part is the bit to use. Trim the end and slice finely. One average blade or stalk should give about 2 tablespoons finely sliced lemon grass. Alternatively, the whole stalk can be bashed hard with a knife handle to release all the flavour and then added while cooking; don't forget to take it out before serving. Stalks will last for about 2–3 weeks in the refrigerator.

Shrimp Paste Made from prawns and salt that have been allowed to ferment and then mashed to a paste. Can be bought in Oriental stores. This is very pungent and salty and used in small amounts. Anchovy paste may be used as a substitute.

Soy Bean Paste A Japanese seasoning mix made from fermented soy beans. There are different varieties depending on what has been added to the soy bean, for example: rice miso, kome-miso, barley miso/mugi-miso, and ordinary soy bean miso/mame-miso. Available in Oriental stores.

Stocks Home-made stocks – chicken, beef or vegetable – impart a marvellous flavour to soups, stews and sauce alike, and they're simple and satisfying to make. But don't forget to skim them well. You can also buy the ready-made liquid variety from many delicatessens and supermarkets.

Tamarind Tamarind is the dried fruit of the tamarind tree, native to East Africa. It is sometimes called an Indian date because the tree is grown all over India and the fruit has a sticky appearance. It has a sharp, acidic taste. The pods are allowed to mature on the tree until the flesh turns dark brown and soft. They are then shelled and maybe seeded and sold in sticky brown blocks of tamarind pulp, which has to be made into tamarind water before using. To do this you have to soak 25 g/1 oz pulp in 300 ml (½ pint) hot water, stir and leave for between 5–30 minutes. The longer the tamarind is left to soak, the stronger the flavour. The amount of tamarind pulp and water can be adjusted to the thickness required for the recipe. The tamarind water is strained off pressing as much out of the pulp as possible. The pulp is discarded.

Tamarind paste or concentrate is available from Asian stores and is ready to use. It is simply mixed with stock or water or even added directly to the dish. It does not need straining and again may be used in different strengths according to the recipe.

Tang Chi This is preserved radish, sold whole or in slices in vacuum-sealed packs. It is used chopped small, to add texture and flavour. Available from Chinese or Oriental stores.

PENGUIN 60s

ISABEL ALLENDE · *Voices in My Ear*
NICHOLSON BAKER · *Playing Trombone*
LINDSEY BAREHAM · *The Little Book of Big Soups*
KAREN BLIXEN · *From the Ngong Hills*
DIRK BOGARDE · *Coming of Age*
ANTHONY BURGESS · *Childhood*
ANGELA CARTER · *Lizzie Borden*
CARLOS CASTANEDA · *The Sorcerer's Ring of Power*
ELIZABETH DAVID · *Peperonata and Other Italian Dishes*
RICHARD DAWKINS · *The Pocket Watchmaker*
GERALD DURRELL · *The Pageant of Fireflies*
RICHARD ELLMANN · *The Trial of Oscar Wilde*
EPICURUS · *Letter on Happiness*
MARIANNE FAITHFULL · *Year One*
KEITH FLOYD · *Hot and Spicy Floyd*
ALEXANDER FRATER · *Where the Dawn Comes Up Like Thunder*
ESTHER FREUD · *Meeting Bilal*
JOHN KENNETH GALBRAITH · *The Culture of Contentment*
ROB GRANT AND DOUG NAYLOR · *Scenes from the Dwarf*
ROBERT GRAVES · *The Gods of Olympus*
JANE GRIGSON · *Puddings*
SOPHIE GRIGSON · *From Sophie's Table*
KATHARINE HEPBURN · *Little Me*
SUSAN HILL · *The Badness Within Him*
ALAN HOLLINGHURST · *Adventures Underground*
BARRY HUMPHRIES · *Less is More Please*
HOWARD JACOBSON · *Expulsion from Paradise*
P. D. JAMES · *The Girl Who Loved Graveyards*
STEPHEN KING · *Umney's Last Case*
LAO TZU · *Tao Te Ching*
DAVID LEAVITT · *Chips Is Here*

PENGUIN 60s

READ MORE IN PENGUIN

For complete information about books available from Penguin and how to order them, please write to us at the appropriate address below. Please note that for copyright reasons the selection of books varies from country to country.

IN THE UNITED KINGDOM: Please write to *Dept. EP, Penguin Books Ltd, Bath Road, Harmondsworth, Middlesex UB7 ODA.*

IN THE UNITED STATES: Please write to *Consumer Sales, Penguin USA, P.O. Box 999, Dept. 17109, Bergenfield, New Jersey 07621-0120.* VISA and MasterCard holders call 1-800-253-6476 to order Penguin titles.

IN CANADA: Please write to *Penguin Books Canada Ltd, 10 Alcorn Avenue, Suite 300, Toronto, Ontario M4V 3B2.*

IN AUSTRALIA: Please write to *Penguin Books Australia Ltd, P.O. Box 257, Ringwood, Victoria 3134.*

IN NEW ZEALAND: Please write to *Penguin Books (NZ) Ltd, Private Bag 102902, North Shore Mail Centre, Auckland 10.*

IN INDIA: Please write to *Penguin Books India Pvt Ltd, 706 Eros Apartments, 56 Nehru Place, New Delhi 110 019.*

IN THE NETHERLANDS: Please write to *Penguin Books Netherlands bv, Postbus 3507, NL-1001 AH Amsterdam.*

IN GERMANY: Please write to *Penguin Books Deutschland GmbH, Metzlerstrasse 26, 60594 Frankfurt am Main.*

IN SPAIN: Please write to *Penguin Books S. A., Bravo Murillo 19, 1° B, 28015 Madrid.*

IN ITALY: Please write to *Penguin Italia s.r.l., Via Felice Casati 20, I-20124 Milano.*

IN FRANCE: Please write to *Penguin France S. A., 17 rue Lejeune, F-31000 Toulouse.*

IN JAPAN: Please write to *Penguin Books Japan, Ishikiribashi Building, 2-5-4, Suido, Bunkyo-ku, Tokyo 112.*

IN GREECE: Please write to *Penguin Hellas Ltd, Dimocritou 3, GR-106 71 Athens.*

IN SOUTH AFRICA: Please write to *Longman Penguin Southern Africa (Pty) Ltd, Private Bag X08, Bertsham 2013.*